Do You KNOW?™

GOLF

A challenging quiz for anyone who loves
the world's greatest game

Guy Robinson

SOURCEBOOKS, INC.®
NAPERVILLE, ILLINOIS

Published by Sourcebooks, Inc.
P.O. Box 4410, Naperville, Illinois 60567-4410
(630) 961-3900
Fax: (630) 961-2168
www.sourcebooks.com

ISBN-13: 978-1-4022-1455-4
ISBN-10: 1-4022-1455-3

Printed and bound in the United States of America
SP 10 9 8 7 6 5 4 3 2 1

You may hit the links only occasionally or live and breathe the game. You may be a hopeless duffer or a serious trophy winner (or somewhere in the vast in-between). You may simply look in on a tournament now and then or have your TV remote permanently fixed on The Golf Channel. But wherever your position on the golf spectrum, no doubt you've learned a fair amount about the game, from watching, reading, and listening to golf people do what they do best: talk about golf.

This book will test that bank of knowledge, quizzing you on some of the rules of the game, the stars of yesterday and today, great moments in great tournaments, courses here and abroad, the equipment, golf in the movies, golf on the moon, and more. Some are easy, some are hard, and the range of topics is very broad. You can be sure you won't answer them all, and you'll learn something in trying.

So here are 100 questions. Count ten points for each correct answer. Where a question has more than one part, you'll be told how to divide the credit. Here and there you'll find a chance to earn five or ten bonus points, so it's theoretically possible to score more than 1,000. (But you won't!)

Figure your performance this way:

Above 900:	**Spectacular!**
700–899:	A very solid showing
500–699:	Nothing to be ashamed of
Below 500:	Told you it was tough

1. Of the four major men's golf championship events, only the Masters is held on the same course every year. That course:

_____

2. Besides cash and a sterling silver replica of the Masters trophy, the winner gets to wear a certain article of clothing for a year, passed along by the previous year's recipient in the manner of a Miss America crowning. What garment, and what color, is it?

_____

3. Mark Twain may or may not have said that "Golf is a good walk spoiled," but it's a nice line anyway. Here are two other fine quotations about the game. For five points each, who's speaking?

   a. "I'll shoot my age if I have to live to be 105." (He almost made it; he was an old-time comedian who had a PGA tournament named for him and is in the World Golf Hall of Fame) B_____ H_____
   b. "I'm the best. I just haven't played yet." (A world-famous sports figure) M_____ A_____

4. At what age do players become eligible for the Champions Tour?

   a. 50
   b. 52
   c. 55
   d. 62

5. Bill and Melinda Gates were married on New Year's Day 1994. Where?

_____

6. First was a guy called Fluff. Then came a New Zealander named Steve. Explain.

_____

7. I'm known for my nonstop chatter on the links. People say I used to golf with a Coke bottle taped and tied to a tree branch just to hustle the country club golfers. I once wore a bandage on my arm to cover the tattoo that spelled the name of my ex-wife. (Later I had the tattoo removed.) If you're a fan of video games, you may know that there's one named after me. I had a cameo in that Adam Sandler movie where he plays a guy who can't make it as a hockey player so he joins the PGA Tour instead. Had enough? Who am I?

8. How many numbered rules are there in the standardly accepted rule book of golf?

    a. 13   c. 99
    b. 34   d. 613

_____

9. Who on this list *hasn't* been honored with a named golf tournament?

a. Bing Crosby
b. Sammy Davis Jr.
c. Frank Sinatra
d. Danny Thomas
e. Glenn Campbell
f. Dinah Shore
g. Gerald R. Ford
h. Alice Cooper

i. Hootie & the Blowfish
j. Halle Berry
k. Michael Jordan
l. Joe Garagiola
m. Ed McMahon
n. Andy Williams
o. The Gatlin Brothers

10. What happens if you sign an incorrect scorecard? Five points for each proper recollection of the rules.

    a. If you sign for a lower score: _____

    b. If you sign for a higher score: _____

11. I'm a top-ranked golfer. As a child, unable to afford golf balls, I practiced with coconuts. I once was suspended from a tour because folks said I dropped a couple of points on my scorecard, but I got past all that. Much later I was accused of making a sexist remark about Annika—Annika Sörenstam, the terrific Swedish champ. Who am I?

_____

12. One of the five founding golf clubs of the United States Golf Association is in Brookline, Massachusetts. It has hosted the Ryder Cup, U.S. Open tournaments, and others. It's called:

    a. The Brookline Golf Club

    b. The Brookline Golf and Country Club

    c. The Clyde & Squirrel Club

    d. The Country Club

13. Where can you find these clubs? Two points each.

    a. Harbour Town Golf Links   f. Charlotte, NC

    b. Quail Hollow Club   g. Tulsa, OK

    c. Winged Foot Golf Club   h. Hilton Head, SC

    d. Southern Hills Country Club   i. Southampton, NY

    e. Shinnecock Hills Golf Club   j. Mamaroneck, NY

14. For several years back in the '70s I was hot on the PGA Tour. Real hot. Now, my playing years behind me, I give my opinions of the golf games of others as a network TV golfcaster. Real opinions, too—for example, I once described a golfer's swing as something that would "make Ben Hogan puke." Who am I?

J _____ M_____

15. Hit it big in the tournament world and you should find your way to plenty of endorsement deals. Here are four lists of products and brands. Three were plugged by big champs of the past (three points apiece for these identifications). The other group is on the resume of a more contemporary golfer (one point for nailing this one).

    a. Coke, L&M cigarettes, Heinz, Lincoln-Mercury, Pennzoil, Rolex
    b. Hathaway, Bostonian, Hart Schaffner & Marx, Pontiac, Magic Chef
    c. Nike, Wheaties, Titleist, Buick, American Express
    d. Bromo Seltzer, Ben Gay, Timex, Pabst Blue Ribbon

16. What, according to the USGA, is the minimum diameter of a golf ball?

    a. 1.50 inches
    b. 1.62 inches
    c. 1.68 inches
    d. 1.99 inches

17. And the maximum weight?

    a. 1.62 ounces
    b. 1.68 ounces
    c. 1.79 ounces
    d. 1.80 ounces

18. And while we're measuring, what about the hole? It must be:

    a. 4 to 5 inches in diameter and 4 to 5 inches deep
    b. 4 to 4½ inches in diameter and 4 to 5 inches deep
    c. 4½ inches in diameter and any depth at all
    d. 4½ inches in diameter and at least 4 inches deep

19. Match the golf term with the definition:

a. snowman
b. the yips
c. looper
d. albatross
e. floating mulligan

f. a caddie
g. a score of eight on a hole
h. a double eagle in Britain
i. nervous twitching before a putt
j. a liberally available do-over

20. Under the rules, whom may you ask for advice during play?

a. Only your caddie
b. Your caddie and your playing partner
c. Your caddie, your partner, and your partner's caddie
d. Anyone, so long as you don't respond audibly

21. In the 15th century, King James II of Scotland banned golf. Why?

_____

22. Can you match the important golfing names with their countries of origin?

a. Peter Thomson
b. Severiano Ballesteros
c. Roberto DeVicenzo
d. Nick Price
e. Marlene Stewart Streit

f. Canada
g. Australia
h. Zimbabwe
i. Spain
j. Argentina

23. Just one of these top golfers *isn't* from South Africa. Which one?

a. Nick Faldo
b. David Frost
c. Ernie Els
d. Bobby Locke
e. Gary Player

24. Tell what these three important figures from the history of golf had in common: Cary Middlecoff (won big in the '40s and '50s), Coburn Haskell (invented the first rubber-core ball), and George C. Grant (held the first patent on a golf tee).

_____

25. This enormously successful pop singer and movie star died in the club locker room right after playing a four-ball in Madrid with British PGA winner Manuel Piñero:
B_____ C_____.

26. Some Tiger miscellany, for two points apiece.

   a. His first name is _____.
   b. He grew up in _____.
   c. His coach early in his career was Butch _____.
   d. He resolved his nearsightedness with _____.
   e. Redesigning courses to make them tougher is called

   _____.

27. Who, at the age of 20, pulled off a stunning upset in the 1913 U.S. Open by defeating two British superstars, Harry Vardon (the premier shot maker of the time) and Ted Ray (the longest hitter)?

   _____

28. For five points each, provide the company names: Big Bertha drivers are made by _____ _____ and PING putters are made by

   _____
   _____.

29. In the pre-metal days, the favored wood for golf club shafts was:

   a. hickory   c. cherry
   b. maple   d. red oak

30. When did the USGA accept the use of golf clubs with steel shafts?

    a. 1926
    b. 1938
    c. 1959
    d. 1980

31. If you know something about these big names in golfing, you probably know their nicknames. Put 'em together, if you can, for two points each.

    a. Ernie Els
    b. Masashi Ozaki
    c. Greg Norman
    d. Ben Hogan
    e. Jack Nicklaus

    f. "Jumbo"
    g. "The Great White Shark"
    h. "The Golden Bear"
    i. "The Hawk"
    j. "The Big Easy"

32. Try five more.

    a. Gene Sarazen
    b. Ky Laffoon
    c. Arnold Palmer
    d. Gary Player
    e. Sam Snead

    f. "The King"
    g. "The Black Knight"
    h. "The Squire"
    i. "The Slammer"
    j. "The Chief"

33. According to the rules, how may you test the putting green?

    a. By rolling the ball in play
    b. By rolling another ball
    c. By rolling any spherical object except a golf ball
    d. None of the above

34. Pick the one president of these five who *didn't* play golf at all:

   a. Clinton
   b. Nixon
   c. Reagan
   d. Carter
   e. Bush Sr.

35. Can you locate the famous holes or features with these popular names? Two points for each proper match-up.

   a. "The Postage Stamp"   f. the 17th at the Old Course, St. Andrews, Scotland
   b. "The Road Hole"   g. around the 12th at Augusta National, Georgia
   c. "Hell's Half Acre"   h. the 8th at the Royal Troon, Scotland
   d. "The Amen Corner"   i. the 3rd at Oakmont Country Club, Pennsylvania
   e. "The Church Pews"   j. the 7th at Pine Valley, New Jersey

36. Jack Nicklaus and Tom Kite are to the interlocking grip as Sam Snead and Nick Faldo are to the _____ grip.

37. I won the New Mexico Women's Amateur title when I was 12. I had a fine amateur career, and when I went pro I won Rookie of the Year and Player of the Year in the same season. I'm married to Ray Knight, the former Mets third baseman whose claim to fame is that he scored the winning run against the Red Sox in Game 6 of the '86 World Series on Mookie Wilson's grounder through Bill Buckner's legs. Who am I?

_____

38. The names Jones, MacDonald, and Fazio are all connected with the field of:

_____

39. Both the Callaway and Peoria systems of one-day handicapping plug a player's performance in a completed round into a formula to determine an adjusted score. In the two systems, which holes in the round are used?

    a. Callaway: _____
    b. Peoria: _____

40. How many holes are typically found on a miniature golf course?

    a. 3 or 6
    b. 9 or 18
    c. 24
    d. 25

41. For two points each, match the golfers with the characteristics of their games.

    a. Cary Middlecoff   f. short swing
    b. Doug Sanders   g. deep concentration
    c. Joyce Wethered (Lady Heathcoate-Amory)   h. long drives
    d. Billy Casper   i. excruciatingly slow play
    e. John Daly   j. putting with the wrists

42. Arrange the following wedges in order of increasing loft:

    a. gap wedge
    b. lob wedge
    c. pitching wedge
    d. sand wedge

43. You want to play a shot from your knees, but the grass is wet, so you drop a towel on the ground to keep your trousers dry. OK?

    a. OK
    b. OK if you shoot and remove the towel within 60 seconds
    c. OK if the towel is no larger than 100 cm in perimeter
    d. Not OK

44. Harvey Penick, the much admired golf teacher, wrote and sold a lot of copies of *Harvey Penick's* _____ _____ _____.

45. And the book *Five Lessons: The Modern Fundamentals of Golf*—who wrote that one?

_____

46. In what year did the Boy Scouts of America first offer a merit badge in golf?

    a. 1912
    b. 1945
    c. 1956
    d. 1977

47. A pair of firsts. Five points for each golfer's name:

    a. First African-American to win a PGA Tour event, 1969:
      C_____
      S_____ .
    b. First African-American to play at the Masters, 1975:
      L_____ E_____ .

48. It's a big, big three-day event with teams from Europe and the U.S. In the 1999 edition, the Americans lagged until nearly the end, then leapt to a stirring come-from-behind win. Justin Leonard's 45-foot putt was the magic. The event's name, please?

_____

49. The Masters Tournament was put on the map back in 1935, its second year, by a famous "miracle shot" on the 15th at Augusta, a par 4 that was double-eagled. By whom?

_____

50. I'm Australian-born, one of the leading female golfers in the world. At 30 I became the youngest living person ever inducted into the Golf Hall of Fame. David Duval and I once teamed up to play Tiger and Annika in an alternate-shot competition; they won. Enough hints? Who am I?

_____

51. Two more fun golf quotes. Five points for each ID.

   a. "I know I'm getting better at golf. I'm hitting fewer spectators." (A U. S. President) G_____ F_____
   b. "It took me 17 years to get 3,000 hits in baseball. I did it in one afternoon on the golf course." (One of baseball's greats)
   H_____ A_____

52. What's the penalty for employing more than one caddie at a time?

   a. Disqualification
   b. Replaying the entire round
   c. Two strokes for each hole for which the extra caddie provided any function
   d. No penalty

53. A best-guess estimate of the number of golf courses in the world is about:

   a. 8,000
   b. 35,000
   c. 80,000
   d. 300,000

54. What does "R&A" stand for?

_____

55. The first American-born player to win the British Open, I was one of the dominant golfers of my time, credited with turning pro golf into a real business. Still, for all my interest in the money end of things I once said, "Never hurry, never worry, and be sure to smell the flowers along the way." Who was I?

_____

56 In one installment of a long-running TV sitcom, a character drives golf balls into the ocean. One of them becomes lodged in a whale's blowhole and the whale nearly dies. Who saves the beached whale?

G_____ C_____

57. Who were the early Scottish golf stars known as "Old Tom" and "Young Tom"?

_____

58 What are a cleek, a mashie, and a niblick? Be precise, please.

_____

59. What penalty is imposed when the ball collides with an unattended flagstick?

    a. one stroke
    b. two strokes
    c. three strokes
    d. mandatory do-over

60. By USGA regulation, how many dimples are allowed on a regulation golf ball?

_____

61. Who was injured by lightning at the 1975 Western Open?

62. And what golf great was severely injured in a run-in with a bus in 1949, but recovered and kept on winning?

63. A film biography was made about that golfer's accident and comeback. Glenn Ford played the golfer, Anne Baxter his wife. Jimmy Demaret, Sam Snead, and Cary Middlecoff appeared as themselves. The movie's title, please.

64. What's the popular name of the Golf Champion Trophy, the winner's cup at the British Open? (Five-point bonus: By tradition, what does the winner do with the trophy upon receipt?)

65. Bobby Jones was one of the very top amateurs of all time, winning both the U.S. and British Opens in 1926 and astounding the golf world with a Grand Slam in 1930. At age 28, he formally retired from competition and devoted his time to his day job. What job was that?

   a. writer
   b. chiropractor
   c. golf ball manufacturer
   d. lawyer

66. The first golf course and club in the U.S. was built in Yonkers, New York, in:

    a. 1856
    b. 1866
    c. 1888
    d. 1911

67. They were known as Arnie's Army? Who were they?

    _____

    _____

68. In 1965, at the Greater Greensboro Open, Sam Snead became the oldest winner of a PGA Tour event. At what age?_____

69. Golfers Tony Lema and Payne Stewart both died the same way. How?

_____

70. Who may invoke winter rules?

    a. Only the local club
    b. The local club or a majority of the golfers involved
    c. The local club *and* a majority of the golfers involved, in agreement
    d. The first golfer to arrive at the first tee

71. Idiosyncrasies? Unusual habits? Plenty of those on the golf course, to be sure. Two points for each match.

    a. Wears red shirt on tournament's last day   f. Gary Player
    b. Wears all black   g. Mickey Wright
    c. Wears tennis shoes, not golf footwear   h. Tiger Woods
    d. Wears colorful outfits   i. Jimmy Demaret
    e. Performs mock sword play with putter   j. Chi Chi Rodriguez

72. I won quite a few major championships, including the U.S. and British Opens in the same year, 1982. I've done course designing. I resigned from my hometown club to protest its exclusionary membership practices. Who am I?

T_____ W_____

73. Baseball had Babe Ruth. Golf had Babe Didrikson Zaharias, possibly the most popular female golfer ever. But Babe did more than golf. She was, among other things, an Olympic medalist—gold in two sports, silver in another—and she also excelled in a long list of other sports. Which of these *didn't* she do?

    a. Swimming
    b. Squash
    c. Tennis
    d. Speed skating
    e. Basketball
    f. Cycling
    g. Baseball
    h. Softball
    i. Bowling
    j. Billiards

74. Who or what was Iron Byron, and why the name?

    _____

75. Who called his putter "Calamity Jane"?

    a. Nick Faldo
    b. Ben Crenshaw
    c. Bobby Jones
    d. Tarzan

76. In which James Bond movie does Bond catch his golfing opponent cheating? (Ten bonus points if you know where the golfing scene was filmed.)

_____

77. At baseball, he was a master; at golf, less so. But at both sports, he was a pro when it came to saying things that would make you laugh. On one occasion on the links, when he complained that his shot was going to go into the water, his golfing partner urged, "C'mon, think positive." "OK," he replied, "I'm positive my shot is going into the water." Who was he?

_____

78. Which circumstance can officially stop a game?

    a. Rain sufficient to require steady use of auto windshield wipers
    b. Snow at a rate greater than one inch per hour
    c. Wind at a speed greater than 40 miles per hour
    d. Hailstones greater than $\frac{1}{4}$ inch in circumference
    e. Lightning

79. Under the rules, when is a ball declared lost?

    a. When the player and at least three co-players or observers agree to halt the search
    b. After five minutes of searching
    c. After nine minutes of searching
    d. After "a reasonable time" has been invested in the search

80. Name the important British golf writer who covered the golf scene for decades and was the grandson of a great naturalist.

B_____
D_____

81. Name the astronaut who hit golf balls on the moon on February 6, 1971.

_____

82. What Japanese player lost a ball in a tree in the rough, ultimately costing him the '87 U.S. Open at the Olympic Club in San Francisco? (Bonus: Ten points if you can repeat the comment he made later.)

T_____ N_____

83. For five points apiece, in which of the 50 states can you find these courses?

  a. Witch Hollow Course: _____
  b. The "Blue Monster": _____

84. We were a couple of British sisters, Harriot and Margaret, who between us in the early 1900s won the U.S. Women's Amateur Golf Championship four times. A famous amateur women's team competition was named for us. What was our last name?

_____

85. Michelle Wie was born in:

  a. Seoul
  b. Panmunjom
  c. Honolulu
  d. Sacramento

86. I'm a one-time college football star who turned pro golfer and won the U.S. Open three times, the last at age 45. Once I turned senior, I may as well have been coining money with all my wins on the Champions Tour. My nephew was a college football success too, but he went pro in football, not golf, playing guard for the Patriots, the Dolphins, and the Rams. Who am I?

H_____ I_____

87. The course has only four holes with their own greens; the rest all share two holes to a green. It has 112 bunkers. It's closed to golfers on Sundays, when it becomes a park for locals to stroll and picnic. It's considered the world's oldest golf club. Name that course.

_____

88. Which U.S. Supreme Court justice, while in office, scored a hole-in-one at the Paradise Valley Country Club in Arizona?

    a. Clarence Thomas
    b. Louis Brandeis
    c. David Souter
    d. Sandra Day O'Connor

89. Tom Weiskopf, like so many others, will vouch for it: The 12th hole at Augusta can be a killer. When he played the 1980 Masters, he set a tournament record by running the hole to _____ strokes.

90. Which former vice president has had *two* aces? (Hint: It's the same vice president who was accused by a female lobbyist of inappropriate behavior toward her during a golfing weekend, and whose wife defended him by saying, "Anyone who knows _____ _____ knows he'd rather play golf than have sex any day.")

91. Another golfing politician—a president of the United States, in fact—was interrupted on the first tee by reporters asking about an attack in Israel that had killed nine bus passengers. Said the president: "I call upon all nations to do everything they can to stop these terrorist killers. Thank you. Now watch this drive." Which president?

_____

92. What connects Bob Charles, Mike Weir, and Phil Mickelson?

_____

93. It's one of the most expensive courses in the world, with smashing views of the Pacific coast, and is a frequent host of major tournaments, including several U.S. Opens. Golfers often call it simply "Pebble Beach." What's its proper name?

    a. Pebble Beach Golf Club
    b. Pebble Beach Golf Links
    c. Pebble Beach Courses
    d. Golf at Pebble Beach

94. What 1980 film comedy portrays fun and games on the links at "Bushwood Country Club"? (Hint: Think Rodney Dangerfield, Bill Murray, Chevy Chase, and the like.)

_____

95. I'm known for my regular discussion shows on The Golf Channel, and for doing impressions of other golfers. Oh, and I have a nice bunch of PGA and Champions Tour wins to my credit. Who am I?

    P _____ J _____

96. How many times has Jack Nicklaus won the Canadian Open?

    a. Once
    b. Twice
    c. Thrice
    d. Zero

97. Two of these golfing figures have appeared on United States postage stamps. One hasn't. For five points each, pick the two who have.

    a. Bobby Jones
    b. Francis Ouimet
    c. Walter Hagen

98. Name the 1980s two-time PGA Tour winner, now a leading instructor, who plays righty but can also handle himself well as a southpaw.

_____

99. The tale of the Masters 1968, 17th hole, is high on everyone's short list of the most distressing bloopers in tournament history: X's playing partner, Y, marks 4 for the hole on X's scorecard instead of the birdie 3 he actually made. At the end, X has shot a 65 but the scorecard reads 66. X misses the mistake and signs the card, so under the rules, the flub must stand. Z, with a 65, is declared tournament winner. Who's X? (For five more points, who's Z? For ten more, who's Y?)

_____

100. Here's a bit of dialogue you may have encountered—more than once if you're much of a TV watcher. Finish the last line. The scene opens with "E" reading from an instruction book:

    E: "'The golf swing. First, step up, plant your feet firmly on the ground, and address the ball.'"
    R: "Wait a minute. What do they mean by 'address the ball'?"
    E: "How should I know? That's what it says here."
    R: "Well, read a little further. Maybe it explains it."
    E: "Umm…ummmm… no, that's all it says: 'address the ball.'… Wait a minute—I think I know what it means there. Here, give me the club… Step up…plant your feet firmly…_____ _____!"

ANSWERS

1. Augusta National Golf Club

2. A green sports jacket

3. a. Bob Hope, b. Muhammad Ali

4. a.

5. On the 12th tee at The Challenge at Manele golf course, on the island of Lana'i, off the west coast of Maui in Hawaii

6. Mike "Fluff" Cowan caddied for Tiger Woods from 1996 to 1999; he was replaced by Steve Williams

7. Lee Trevino (the video game is *Lee Trevino's Fighting Golf*; the movie is the sports comedy *Happy Gilmore*)

8. b.

9. No one

10. a. You're disqualified, b. You're stuck with it

11. Vijay Singh

12. d.

13. a.-h., b.-f., c.-j., d.-g., e.-i.

14. Johnny Miller

15. a. Arnold Palmer (3 pts.), b. Jack Nicklaus (3 pts.), c. Tiger Woods (1 pt.), d. Ben Hogan (3 pts.)

16. c.

17. a.

18. d.

19. a.-g., b.-i., c.-f., d.-h., e.-j.

20. c.

21. Because golf was distracting young men of the time from their archery practice, which was needed for national defense; 45 years later, the ban was lifted by James IV

22. a.-g., b.-i., c.-j., d.-h., e.-f.

23. a. (Faldo is English)

24. Each was a dentist

25. Bing Crosby

26. a. Eldrick, b. California, c. Harmon, d. laser surgery, e. Tiger-proofing

27. Francis Ouimet

28. Callaway Golf and Karsten Manufacturing

29. a.

30. a.

31. a.–j., b.–f., c.–g., d.–i., e.–h.

32. a.–h., b.–j., c.–f., d.–g., e.–i.

33. d.

34. d.

35. a.–h., b.–f., c.–j., d.–g., e.–i.

36. The Vardon (overlapping) grip

37. Nancy Lopez

38. Golf course design

39. a. all the holes, b. six ones (which ones to be used not announced until after play)

40. b.

41. a.–i., b.–f., c.–g., d.–j., e.–h.

42. c., a., d., b.

43. d.

44. *Little Red Book*

45. Ben Hogan

46. d.

47. a. Charles Sifford, b. Lee Elder

48. The Ryder Cup

49. Gene Sarazen

50. Karrie Webb

51. a. Gerald Ford, b. Hank Aaron

52. a.

53. b.

54. Royal and Ancient Golf Club of Scotland

55. Walter Hagen

56. In an episode of *Seinfeld*, Kramer drives the ball; George Costanza, pretending to be a marine biologist, retrieves it to save the whale

57. Tom Morris, who was greenskeeper for St. Andrews Links and a major golfer and course designer, and Tom Morris Jr., who won several major tournaments before he died at age 24

58. Old names for a 1-iron, a 5-iron, and a 9-iron

59. b.

60. There's no regulation on this; most golf balls have in the range of 300 to 450

61. Lee Trevino

62. Ben Hogan

63. *Follow the Sun*

64. The Claret Jug (bonus: kisses it)

65. d.

66. c.

67. Arnold Palmer's groupies—fans who followed him from tournament to tournament

68. Nearly 53

69. In a plane crash (Lema in 1966, Stewart in 1999)

70. a.

71. a.-h., b.-f., c.-g., d.-i., e.-j.

72. Tom Watson

73. She did 'em all (in baseball, she once hit five home runs in a single game; why do you think she was called "Babe"?)

74. The USGA's one-armed mechanical device for testing golf balls and clubs, designed to mimic the classic swing of Byron Nelson and named for him

75. c.

76. *Goldfinger*, in which Bond plays Auric Goldfinger for a brick of gold (bonus: Stoke Park Club, outside London)

77. Yogi Berra

78. e.

79. b.

80. Bernard Darwin

81. On the lunar surface, Apollo 14 commander Alan B. Shepard Jr. took three swings at a golf ball using the head of 6-iron strapped to a makeshift shaft; his first try topped the ball and buried it, the second produced a dribble of a few feet, and the third sent the ball flying to who knows where; he repeated with a second ball, again sending it out of sight; as a variation of Shepard's stroke, in 2006, a Russian cosmonaut on a spacewalk near the international space station launched a super-lightweight golf ball into orbit for a few days to promote a Canadian golf club maker

82. Tommy Nakajima (bonus: "That's golf!")

83. a. Pumpkin Ridge Golf Course, Oregon; b. Doral Golf Resort & Spa, Florida

84. Curtis (as in the every-other-year Curtis Cup Match)

85. c.

86. Hale Irwin (uncle of Heath Irwin)

87. The Old Course at St. Andrews, Scotland

88. d.

89. 13

90. Dan Quayle

91. George W. Bush

92. Each plays left-handed

93. b.

94. *Caddieshack*

95. Peter Jacobsen

96. d.

97. a. and b.

98. Mac O'Grady

99. X is Roberto DeVicenzo (who later was given an award for sportsmanship); Y is Tommy Aaron; Z is Bob Goalby

100. "Helloooo, ball!" (Art Carney as Ed Norton, to Jackie Gleason as Ralph Kramden, on *The Honeymooners*)